BROW HEAD

———

John Boland

Abbey Press

First published in May 1999 in an edition of 1,000 copies
including a special limited edition hardback of 250 copies
signed and numbered by the author

Abbey Press
Newry Office
Courtenay Hill
Newry
County Down
Northern Ireland
BT34 2ED

◆

Abbey Press
Belfast Office
24 Martello Park
Craigavad
County Down
Northern Ireland
BT18 0DG

A CIP record for this book is available from the British Library

ISBN: 1 901617 12 2 *paperback*
1 901617 13 0 *hardback*
Author: Boland, John
Title: Brow Head
Format: 138 mm x 214 mm
1999

Design: Adrian Rice
Typesetting by David Anderson in 11/13pt Sabon
Printed by Nicholson & Bass Ltd, Belfast

for

Marlene & Helen

CONTENTS

One might in turn become less diffident,
Out of such mildew plucking neater mould
And spouting new orations of the cold.
One might. One might. But time will not relent.

Wallace Stevens
('The man whose pharynx was bad')

I have always an idea in my mind, a
certain confused picture, which shows
me, as in a dream, a better form than I
have used; but I cannot grasp it.

Montaigne
('On Presumption')

THE HOMING PIGEON

I am an embarrassment to my profession.
I seek a kind of liberty.
My instincts overpower my training.
Released each time from bondage,
I listen dutifully, obediently,
my eyes riveted on my destination.

But once out of cage, of hand, of sight,
I fly free. Look, they have instructed me,
make for Putney (or Donegal, or Normandy),
and a message which means something to someone
is strapped to my leg (the ignominy!).
But instead I fly to Siam
because I have never been to Siam
and it is something new,
and I drop the message in the sea.

Some day, no doubt, they'll find out,
they'll catch me, I'll be kept at home,
my feathers plucked, in disgrace.
But I will wait for my luck to run out.

What I am doing is strictly for the birds.

HELVICK HEAD, 4 MAY
for Joe Kennedy

Out there, on that rock
licked by the waves,
life is pampering itself:

a solitary cormorant
spreads his great wings
to embrace the heat;

nearby, six guillemots,
stunned by the sun,
preen like a foreign legion

waiting to be inspected.
These creatures are wiser
than we are, who have spent

all afternoon struggling
through gorse, tearing
our clothes, risking

our necks, on the off-chance
that we'll be privileged
to see such self-absorption.

THE DEATH OF THE MOTH

Margaret found you
at the side of the house
in a tray full of rain.

You were too exhausted
to flutter free,
so she brought you in

and put you carefully
on the window sill,
to recover your strength.

But you didn't.
The next morning we went
to remove your corpse

and found behind you
fourteen tiny eggs,
a legacy of defiance.

THE SINGER

Snug in this midnight bar, two drinks
in front of him, he bends my ear.
Time to take stock, he thinks:
sixty (can you believe?) this year.

Women, I'm told, once swooned.
He was the baby of the group, though
now his cherub's face, unruined
by all the bad that living throws

at everybody else, looks odd:
you feel it hasn't paid its dues.
Others, it says, can suffer for the god
of art and music if they choose,

he's not a one given to fretting;
women and drink may well cause harm,
but only if you're letting
them get to you. He has a charm,

no doubt, and talent, too, though now
(landlord, the same again!) he wonders
what new approach will best allow
his gifts shine through. There were blunders,

he concedes, down through the years –
maybe too many good times, too –
but what the hell, this fresh career
will show the doubters he's not through.

Closing his eyes, lost in a trance,
he suddenly begins to croon.
This song's for me, all wild romance
and blighted love and death come soon.

His breath is on my face. I blink
and wish that I were elsewhere. Yet
in his past, adoring girls might think
this was as good as life could get.

THE YELLOW HOUSE

Betjeman lived there,
you know, the most famous
resident of this place

way back then, before
the folk-singer came.
To be honest, I never

much rated him – a bit glib,
the English disease,
though the one about

Dungarvan in the rain
has a kind of fey charm.
Yes, I know a thing or two

about poetry: just because
you're a fisherman
doesn't mean you can't read.

But that was all a front,
the teddy bears and writing,
he was down here working

for his London masters,
files on strategic ports,
and stuff like that.

Well, as I've always said,
don't ever trust the British,
especially when they're saying

something else. Mark my words
on this peace and friendship thing,
it's not over yet, not until

the last manjack of them leaves.
Still, can't be blathering
all day, mind how you go.

HEYTESBURY LANE

Waking at night
I hear a pig squeal.

My room is low-ceilinged
with half-moon windows.
Outside the front door
there is a courtyard.
On summer mornings
I can trap the sun.

Sometimes at night, though,
I wake to hear
the pitiable scream
of a trapped pig.
It is difficult to believe
I am not having a nightmare.

When I rise
in the late morning
there is a stillness
in the lane.
I stroll to the shops
past painted doors,
pointed façades,
ladies with toy dogs.
The lane hovers in the heat.

But it is not a nightmare,
this squealing of a pig.
Someone on this lane
is keeping a pig.
All that wealth,
that sobriety!
It is almost comic,
this strange hobby,

except that the animal
seems to be in terror,
bewilderment and outrage,
as if waiting
to be slaughtered,
and I cannot sleep.

THE SCALD CROW
for Emmanuel and Attracta

This particular gent
we have watched
for two years now.

Scavenging on the headland
he'll gobble down
whatever grabs his eye

(maggots, hedgehogs,
chewed drumsticks
in their deli boxes

thrown from cars),
but recently new people
and their friends

have taken the cottage
nearest to the summit.
So each fresh morning

our feathered friend
finds on the gate-post
overlooking the Atlantic

fascinating scraps:
canard a l'orange,
Parma ham, a *daube*,

stale garlic bread
and grated Emmenthal,
left by good people,

mindful of ecology,
and wishing to preserve
the balance of nature.

LUSISTI SATIS

Children are children, so you never think.
Once it was you, but that was long ago,
days dawdling into days. Now they're not slow,
years scream at years, the shaping link

mislaid for ever. Still, you remember
little things. The immensity of it all:
the car approaching and the speckled ball
bouncing, bouncing, catch it, quick; November

and the dying day, a dog scampering
at shadows, blinding blur, the times you had,
watching the world go whooping, yelping, mad;
later in the garden a whimpering,

the car drove on, the white-frocked man is called.
When dogs die do they go to heaven?
Wait till you're older, you'll see it all even
out into nothingness, or mauled

into a shape you never could have dreamed.
Once in an age you're stopped dumb on the stair,
you thought you saw a young girl standing there,
conjuring a life your wide world's never schemed.

GOD IS THE CONCEPT
BY WHICH WE MEASURE OUR PAIN

I don't know. Love may be the pain
by which we measure poetry.
There is an almost infinite series. Anyway,

there was less than feeling
in the way the leaves hung yesterday,
and in the traffic's unconcern
at how they fell, finally, falling slowly.

I was guilty of noticing these things.
No doubt you noticed other things
as we walked by the canal.
I had never before observed
how silently leaves fall,
how undemonstratively they reach the ground.
No wonder people walk on them.

Poetry is the final reply to the abstract.
All passings leave the observer a little wiser.
Poetry is the distillation of all this.
There is a poem to be written sometime
on how, moving along by the canal,
we ignored the larger issues.
Perhaps it is that there is only one season
in which leaves can fall. I don't know.

THE PALACE OF WISDOM

The work is bearable, and I misspend
my allotment. That's not all. One's friends
are necessarily few. I never meet
that many in the day. Not to greet

would be ungracious. Work suffers, though.
There are many truths I cannot know.
One is, how on earth to reconcile
ravings in a room with the half-smile

over a glass of wine. It's not easy.
Something suffers. Someone. Would I please you
if I worried? But I do. There's the rub,
the nub. Someone is waiting. There's the pub.

THE STARS IN THEIR COURSES

Yes, we were lonely, too.

Later we smiled
in the face of the sky,
then turned away,
speaking our speech,
towards the singing room.

Complications followed.

In the end, the world knew.

FOR THOSE WHO WERE NOT THERE

Let's say
that the day was good.

In the morning we walked
close to the river's edge.
Gulls flapped across the water,
the sun created mirrors,
swallows displayed no effort.

In the trees a blackbird
mocked at history.

Time was accommodating.

In the evening
the stars in their courses
requested silence.

We were accommodating.

◆

Let's say
that none of this happened.

I lay on my bed.
The rain was inexhaustible.
In the afternoon I drowsed.

It was a good day.

THROUGH THE VANISHING POINT

You betray your calm
too easily.
No man is worth
this nervousness
of hands.

On your sea rambles
did the ebb-tide
teach you nothing?

Look at the sun.
See, it is part
of the sky.
Take it home
and frame it
on your wall.

When you dampen
under his eyes
the outcome is not
inevitable.
All rooms
are landscapes
with figures.

Listen
to one who knows
the value
of poetry.

IDEAS OF ORDER IN A ROOM IN DUBLIN

There is no terror in the night.
The drunken city curls its paws to sleep.
No bottle breaks. No expletive seeks freedom
in the stars. The streetlamp holds its glow,
illuminating areas. No birds cry.

Grope for the rails, the stairs are dark
with shadows. Here is the room.
Admire the care, absence of bric-a-brac.
You will recall how objects demonstrate
a character: Constable's cathedral,
landscape balanced by spire's symmetry,
holding the walls in place. No doubt
you pause over the books: the titles show
a binding theme, pursuit of pure reason.
The Mozart lends an atmosphere,
catching the room within its form,
the process ultimate, complete. Ignore
the bed: the sheet-stains illustrate
mere marginalia, a rage for privacy.

Ramon Fernandez, tell me, if you know,
where youth and joy and wonder go.

THE OLD SCHOLAR PREPARES
TO SAIL TO BYZANTIUM

Too many nights I stumbled on the stair,
retching the wine out of my blood,
my body spent, brain flicking for order,
for something tangible outside the mind.

Now it is winter. Beyond my window,
rooks gather restlessly, waiting for night,
the orgy before sleep. It will be time
soon to stop reading, light seeps away,

only the eternal verities remain.
The day has had its day, one more reprieve
for lovers and the like; they, too, will move
towards the point where only dreams reside,

they, too, will summarise gains and losses.
My body, disciplined for greater good,
prepares itself for sleep. My tired eyes
find the dark. Was it for this I stayed behind?

GOD SMILED AGAIN

At last we slept,
and in the morning rose
to clear the debris.

I licked my wounds.
It's just we love
not wisely but too well,
you pleaded,

and recalled that afterwards
we sought redemption,
framed by the fire
inside a kindly room.

We purged our guilt, you said.
I almost screamed.
I never wanted
to be a romantic poet.

Let us recall:
God did not smile again,
there was no sudden
singing in the sky.

We fought, teeth, hair, blood,
the customary scene.

Later I stroked you
till you fell asunder.
Let's leave out love
and call it plunder:
in the strict sense
surely an indictable offence.

SUCH STUFF

The dank night dredges up oddities,
flotsam and scum and stuff that bloats,
shapeless, drifting in a black breeze,

scraping the heavy hulls of boats,
straining for the sea, while men fling
ropes ashore for mooring. Ships sound notes

of entry and departure, first greeting
and last farewell. The garbage sways,
directionless, unwanted things,

discarded, having done the day:
a pram, an old tyre, something that gleams,
and then, dimly, further away,

slowly circling, something that seems
too real for words . . . Live with the living!
And think of all those wondrous dreams

trembling for their fulfilment, giving
a passage to the ocean, free
of all but seagulls' screams, loving

and lonely, promising infinities.
Suddenly the night is colder,
the water slurps, a blacker breeze

insinuates a need to shoulder
off the silence and the queer
damp sense of growing older,

with living too fragile for fear,
and shadows which suggest a mere
nothingness is all that's floating here.

DRUMARD
(Clones, October 16, 1972)
for Eugene McCabe

From my window, the field falls away
down to the road and the lake beyond.
Things are quiet. A red setter
scratches its behind against a tree. A grey
morning rises. There is the distant sound
of early birds. Things are better

than they were. Last night we reached the town
and saw the broken glass and dumb faces,
the news not good. A bomb's a fearful thing . . .
it might well have been us who found
ourselves right there . . . hopefully, with God's grace,
he'll live, but he's hurt bad . . . yes, bad times bring

bad deeds . . . So the murmur goes. Later,
in this house which might have once contained
poor Uncle Vanya, talk should have been a pleasure.
Our references reached out to Walter Pater,
drinks were sipped, aspirations explained,
pleasant, polite people at their leisure.

And none of us would countenance the gloom
that lurked behind our amiable chatter,
of chaos uncomprehended,
not comprehending us; then, in my room,
every sound in the dark seemed to matter
more than it should, the night hardly ended.

In the morning air, the fields look the same
as anywhere, always; while in the town there's a force
of green recruits. Out of such things I fashion poems,
spending my hours searching for words that rhyme.
No, that's too cynical, too glib, of course,
but there are times when that's just what it seems.

IN TIME OF 'THE BREAKING OF NATIONS'
(May 17, 1974)

There will be a lovely quiet on our farm,
so hushed we will hear the grass growing
as we saunter down through the cornfield,
make love by the stream where the salmon leap.

Oh, we'll be happy, the two of us,
shouldering home the silence in the evening sun.
The mad and lazy days will never end
and you and I will have such memories.

Somehow we'll have outlived all the rest
and I shall be surrounded by the startling heat,
full of wonder as you in your print frock
are walking towards me infinitely.

INCIDENT AT OWL CREEK
(May 17, 1974)

I am strolling down a field of buttercups.
It is early June, and God is very good.
In the morning it rained; now the sun
is high up in the blue, dangling lazily.

As I walk, my shoes are stained yellow.
A lark breaks from cover. Such peace.
When I cross the stream you will be waiting,
radiant in that dress your mother wore.

The day alters imperceptibly.
Something is happening to the sky:
I don't know, but somehow it has lowered.
I hurry home, eager to see your face.

Sure enough, you stand smiling at the door.
My love, how could we ever be apart?
The mountain, dark and dull, broods over you.
I turn around and stare from where I came.

From the city comes a distant roar.
Is God angry? A smoky pallor hangs
over a bloody sky. It's all so far away.
The birds scream at us from the treetops.

We have made for ourselves a new world here
no-one can destroy. It is our haven
of all that shines out lovely and true.
Why do you stumble when I come towards you?

IDYLL

The dogs behind, I'm running for the trees.
The field wavers, shuddering in a haze
of sickled yellow. From nowhere, a breeze
fondles my hair. I falter, turn around,
breathe in the landscape: a lifetime's days
of perfect summer crowd without a sound,

except, from far away, a yelp, a bark,
and a deep hum hanging over the wood.
I stand transfixed. Startled, a lark
rises, jinking for the blue. Flies moulder,
shred, disintegrate. I feel I should
linger in this place.

                 The day is colder
suddenly. My legs, regardless, will not budge:
I have caught sight of something at the end
of the far field, a figure seen to nudge
aside the trembling waves. It is a girl
in a print frock, gesturing, someone, a friend,
so far away, arms out. I blink, and worlds whirl

crazily as she, too, whirls, explodes.
Too late, my love, you left it far too long.
I run, reach shadow, where soft moss corrodes
the tangled tree trunks with an ooze of death.
Footsteps pad near. Things have gone madly wrong.
Something approaches. I stop, out of breath.

SUDDENLY, QUITE BY CHANCE

there is a girl undressing
in the house opposite.

I, who have someone of my own,
who undresses nightly, sometimes for me,
stop when I see the lighted window.
My attention is diverted from the gramophone.
A Schubert impromptu is playing.

It is a cold night
and she undresses quickly.
She has forgotten to draw the blinds
(I am not such a fool as to think
she is doing this for me).
Her breasts are very small.
She scratches her bottom
before putting on her nightdress.
She is absorbed in her privacy.
It is really quite beautiful,
this innocence even in the suburbs.

I am too tired to be aroused.
I have been standing too long
in the dark at the window.

THE INFLUENCE OF NATURAL OBJECTS

Love's energy spent,
the room assumes
a new texture.

Come to the window,
look, it is raining.

Five starlings
crystallise the lawn,
wet plumage on fire.

Rising, they wheel,
blurs of insolence,
towards the trees.

A rainbow frames the sky,
streaked with gold
and all the colours
you could name, my love.

Stars emerge.

How could we be
other than happy?

WINTER KEPT US WARM

And then the snow.

We ran inside.
You cried, as I recall,
the tears lingering
longer than the snow
that streaked its sobs
across the window-pane.

The fire laughed,
then we laughed, too,
until laughter and tears
mingled, setting us free
to doubt which was which.

We groped into the dark
as the flames darted and fell.

In the morning
we scattered ashes
down the path's purity
to offset the danger
of falling.

SAFE SEX

Afterwards, from one
or both of you,

will come a whispered
Are you OK?

as if you had just
been in an accident

and were checking
to see who'd survived.

WHAT DO WOMEN WANT?

Everyone says you're the perfect couple.

The rest of us get by after a fashion,
muddling through marriages not made in heaven,
each day unmade by an unkind gesture,
slighting children, and lies that bind
into the years that yawn ahead.

But yours was the one that worked,
and still reproaches us for all we're not.
You holiday abroad to interesting cities,
take weekends in the country when you can,
your bags well stocked with books and compact discs.
At home you're wise enough to know
that privacy's the other side of sharing,
and long since learned that space is freedom.
And though his friends need not be yours,
you like them all (well, not that auctioneer)
and give dinners that are much admired.
Often in bed you both have urgencies;
no problems there. Really, we should hate you.

But we don't. No-one's ever said a bad word
about him, and you're a friend to us all.
Hard, then, to imagine why you choose
three times each month, more if you can,
to go to a room at the top of a stairs
in a house of flats, frayed carpet, faded chairs,
take off your clothes and straddle a man
none of us ever liked. Asked by an anxious friend,
you called it love; to us it's a betrayal.

REPORTS JUST IN

We were the mute observers to the scene,
he was the Serb, you were his Bosnia,
and with dismay we heard the news that came
of raids upon your unprotected zones.

There had been skirmishes down through the years,
and scenes in pubs, where he'd start arguments
and be unpleasant. But this was different,
and from the start we saw the warning signs:

sunglasses that you'd never worn before,
a sudden fad for scarves, things like that.
Still, it was all rather circumstantial,
and it was really none of our business,

and we knew you'd rather if we kept out of it –
confiding wasn't quite your style, and I suppose
you thought that being the busy working mum
would see you through. Finally, though,

he did for you so badly the whole world knew.
We rallied round, but you chose lawyers
rather than friends. Was that so wise?
We hear now that he's trying to make amends.

YOUTH'S A STUFF

Girls I once loved
in this little city
of sexual intrigue

now are married
somewhere out there
among the suburbs.

It was only yesterday
we dawdled for hours
along the Leinster Road

or perched on stools
in dimly-lit bars on
Pembroke Street.

Today I walked
up Grafton Street
and saw how, overnight,

a whole generation
had suddenly turned over.
This evening I lecture

to young Americans,
not the faintest blemish
on those sun-kissed limbs,

their bright smiles
and their wide eyes
stirring vague yearnings.

I feel I know them all,
and am faintly surprised
they don't know me.

THE END OF IT

That moment when
the rituals of love
turn into chores:

the whispered calls
from work desks,
the secret codes

on home phones,
those stolen afternoons
of dazed delirium

out on that bed,
that long-promised weekend
far away from everyone –

all now seem somehow
more difficult to manage,
and in their place

are tiresome problems
you didn't have before
(the office workload,

the family holiday
that this time round
you can't get out of),

and suddenly there you are
in the kitchen
of your empty house,

the half-smoked cigarette
burning itself out,
the milk curdling

in the midday sun,
the phone crying out
for you to call someone.

YOU'LL LIKE MY WIFE

That's what you said, and I did.
The quaint mole up where the thigh
met the drenched tangle of hair,

the sheen of soft fuzz in the curve
of her lower back, the musky smell
as I bowed into her secret self,

these were all much to my liking;
also the way she'd crouch over me,
the better to gobble me down.

You'll like my wife, you said,
she's bright and has a fabulous
sense of humour. That, too.

SEPTEMBER, 1945

in memory of my mother

With a shock I realise I'm in the picture, too.
It is afternoon in the Zoological Gardens
and you are seated on an iron bench, beside
a woman who peers primly at the camera;

behind stands a stern-faced man in a bow-tie,
and next to him my father. You are wearing
a pleated skirt and a simple blouse and jacket.
Your left hand cradles the arm of the bench.

You are not yet thirty and you look boldly out,
daring life to do its worst. It is a Sunday
in the second week of the month and I
(or what will become of me) have been inside you

for three weeks. You're not to know, but in the end
there will be four of us to fill your days
and line your face and, after all is done,
to break a heart run ragged by the years. That's

in the future. For now you are simply on a day out,
recently married to a dark-eyed handsome man
some years your senior, with good prospects
in the civil service. You have an expectant look

as if you can't wait for what each day will bring.
There's no way I can know if you are yet aware
of my existence, or if this day you feel
more proud of me than you'll have cause to be.

THE 62 BUS

Our lives were ruled by the 62 bus.
A phantom service, it came when it wished,
not when the schedule declared – friends
for life were first encountered at the stop.

I took it into work those years I lived
in what my parents chose as their last home,
and peered from the top into suburban gardens,
the trim hedges, fuchsia, forlorn beach balls.

Some nights, with way too many pints on board,
I caught the last one out barely in time,
hoping I wouldn't find my mother at the door.
That's what I mainly miss, I suppose:

her anxious face turning to giddy relief
to see her twenty-year-old smiling drunken son
home in one piece. It is years later now,
and I, too, pace my drawing-room at night,

go to the door and peer out at the dark,
praying my child comes safely home. Meanwhile,
I think of how the 62 took my mother one last time
up to the shops. She complained of a discomfiture.

THE LIFE OF REILLY

My father, who was almost forty-one
when he married my mother, tells me now
that the happiest days he ever spent
were in a boarding house on Gardiner Street.

His present room looks out on a familiar view,
those Dublin mountains he made us climb
when Sunday afternoons meant scenic spins
in a cramped Ford Anglia. I can still see

my mother's eyes raised to timid heaven
each time he stopped for 'one more little walk',
and to this day I tiptoe through the hush
he'd summon later for the Sunday play. And now,

my mother gone, he occupies a bed not made by her
and observes how sixty years ago in a house
on Gardiner Street he had the life of Reilly.
Those are the words he uses. I stare out the window

at the familiar mountains and listen to this man
and his memories of how two spinster ladies
fussed over him as if he were their own,
of his civil service job, his fellow lodgers,

the cheery camaraderie of handball friends,
the pictures every Friday in the Metropole,
that week in Innsbruck when the world was young.
Old enough now to be his father, I watch in rage

as, in another rented room, women fuss over him,
and bring him all he needs, and make him laugh
more than he's done in years. My mother smiles shyly
from his side table as they make his bed.

A PRAYER FOR MY DAUGHTER

Somewhere out there,
further than I can see,
she bobs over the waves,

beyond the blue horizon,
sailing away from me
towards another country.

Less than two hours ago
we wrenched her from her dreams
and drove her down at dawn

to this bleak terminal.
It is nothing, really,
a three-day school outing

to Shakespeare's birthplace,
yet it is a little death,
this first excursion

out on her own. Half woman now
but still half child,
she's needed me to say

those very things
that leave me speechless,
to do what's left undone.

All I can manage is to wish
her troubled soul
some things worth having:

not just love in the heart,
but laughter, ease and peace,
and the wisdom to recognise

whoever or whatever
may bring these gifts to her.
Right now she's somewhere out there,

whispering and giggling
as she nears the other side,
and unaware, I trust,

that the more I dwindle
in her thoughts,
the more she looms in mine.

LULLABY

Just go to sleep, my love,
and don't mind what I said.
Dream of the stars above
and rest your little head.

Tomorrow will be fine
your dad will still be here,
so stop your silly crying
there's nothing you need fear.

Sometimes it's hard, I know,
to tell what life's about,
sometimes we come to blows,
sometimes we have to shout,

but never have I meant
to take it out on you:
you were the one God sent
to show what's good and true.

So go to sleep, my love,
and don't feel any pain.
You are my little dove,
I'll make it right again.

THE LEINSTER ROAD

I have no idea what we talked about
that midsummer bank holiday evening
at the corner of the Leinster Road,

two students circling each other
by the side wall of Rathmines library
and jabbering on as if our lives depended

on it. We didn't know each other then,
and a lifetime later, as I watch you
in the garden from this bedroom window,

I'm only too aware that we still don't.
This, though, was where it all began,
among the sun-specked leaves and shadows

of the Leinster Road, that long journey
towards an accommodation destined to be
always inscrutable, if no longer unfamiliar.

ROAD WORKS AHEAD

The evening grows colder
as we drive towards the city.
There is a chill in its gestures.

I have never seen an evening quite so strange,
it is full of cries and contrasts,
and the ice on the road must be treacherous.
Be careful how you drive.

That bird there, stretched out
beside the cat's eyes,
I think its neck was broken,
there was a bone protruding from its throat.
And those two trees, crouched against the cold,
there's something almost human in their posture.

Ten years ago, in another car,
on this same stretch of road,
we fought, do you remember?
We almost crashed.
And the landscape gathered itself up
and folded itself around us,
and we knew that nature at least was kind.

We have not fought for some time.
As we grow older we manage a kind of balance.

Yet when I look at the sky
I see that the moon is a blood red.
I think it may be angry,
as God is said to be
when one falls from grace.

SAFE JOURNEY

We race into the demon of the night.
A casual flick averts the headlights' glare.
Careless insects, transfixed in flight,
splatter against the glass, their stain
dissolving downwards with the rain.

We have been driving for more than two hours,
the weather worsening. I watch your back
crouched over the wheel, your powers
of concentration fragile in your fingers,
your eyes fixed ahead. Something else lingers

from that night, that drive. There were no tears,
no cries or whispers. We played our parts
as to the drama born, betrayed no fears,
no flutterings impaled upon a glass.
When all is said and done, this is what will last,

two strangers shaped by silence in a car,
not wishing to know why, defining age
as happiness, knowing that they've come far,
maturity at long last settling in.
There have been worse ways to begin.

Later I'm on a bridge, staring down quays.
In all those ghostly faces sloping home
suddenly, without warning, it's you I see,
though oddly you are smiling as you run,
stained by the blood of the evening sun.

AWAY FROM IT ALL
for Steve

Here in Sardinia
on a brief junket,
I soak up the sun,

and listen to a woman
who tells of a love
that came undone,

and there in a golf club
(another brief junket)
somewhere in Sligo,

you sweat in a sauna
on the morning after
a long night before

until life says no more.
I hear it on the news
in the taxi back home,

and recall dawdling over
my continental breakfast
in a heat-drenched square,

while someone in a room
of wood and vapours tries
to give you some more air.

ROUND ABOUT MIDNIGHT

Lights wink from houses up on Dalkey Hill,
the road below my window purrs with cars,
two drunks enact a loony vaudeville,
the moon is full, the sky's agog with stars.

It seems like fun out there, but not to mind;
all round my reading lamp Stan Getz spatters
those soft-blown notes that say the world is kind,
virtue's its own reward, and nothing matters

beyond this sultry samba – such sweet thunder,
and so convincing in its breathy bliss
you'd never think that life could be asunder,
not just in here, where everything's amiss,

but out there, too, for all that I can tell:
the purring from those cars might well be hate,
customised journeys to some private hell;
the house lights on the hill merely a late

doctor on call to a sweat-soaked bed;
that drunken vaudeville spinning to rage
behind closed doors, while a child, misled
from sleep, stumbles upon a ghastly stage.

It needn't be like that, the jazz cajoles,
and those rhapsodic riffs almost persuade
that life is how we shape it, hearts and souls
swaying to a rhythm that will not be unmade.

And so we hunch beneath our lamps and wait:
good times will come, we say, someone will call
and tell us that it still isn't too late
to stop the demons seeping through the wall.

THE WESTERN MYTH
for Peter O'Malley

They have no spilled blood there,
no intoxicating legend of disbelief,
no careless rapture of violence.

With all that rock
there are no monuments;
there are no myths
for rock to glorify.

No doubt the inhabitants do not recognise
their suffocation by prayer and elements,
straitjacketed inside stone walls.
It affords them their freedom, they could say,
but people do not say these things who live there.

It's a good land, a good life, they may nod absently,
tolerant of what you want to hear.
They envisage no other way:
sure, we've lived here always,
what else would we be doing?
Then they shrug and turn away, into the vernacular,
amused at the sergeant's latest quest for poteen:
a man has to prove his identity somehow.

There, one afternoon, two city slickers climbed the only hill
and noticed the slow roll of the Atlantic,
and watched the cumbersome flapping of a heron,
and tried to order the dotted cottages in pattern,
and discovered new meanings to old words,
peace, privacy, civility, words like those.

Here, traffic sounds insist on known meanings.
Here there is no old farmer who believes
that a hill is a hill is a hill
and that that is sufficient.
By the same logic, of course,
a city is a city is a city.
There is no argument.
There is a sense in known meanings.

BROW HEAD

Lost to the world on this finger of land
that claws its way into the open sea,
a village sleeps in the midday heat.

It has been slumbering here a long time,
a clutch of houses convulsed by age
and a century's slow drift to elsewhere.

Children grew up in this place, their kingdom
the fields that run out into the Atlantic,
their roof the sun, the moon and the stars.

No-one now lives within these walls
or leans on half-doors, gazing at a life
the rest of us have long ago forgotten.

We are tourists here, casual daytrippers
content to scavenge around in a ghost town
at the end of the world, dimly disturbed

by something aeons ago in some shared past,
anxious to be started on the journey home.
This is about as far out as we choose to get.

Acknowledgements

Some of these poems first appeared in *Atlantis*, *New Irish Writing*, *The Irish Times* and *Poetry Ireland Review*.

The author wishes to thank John Banville, Gerald Dawe, Seamus Heaney, Brendan Kennelly, David Marcus, Sean O Mordha and Frank Ormsby for helping to make this book possible.